HIPSTER

ADULT COLORING BOOKS

Women and flower designs for relaxation and stress relief

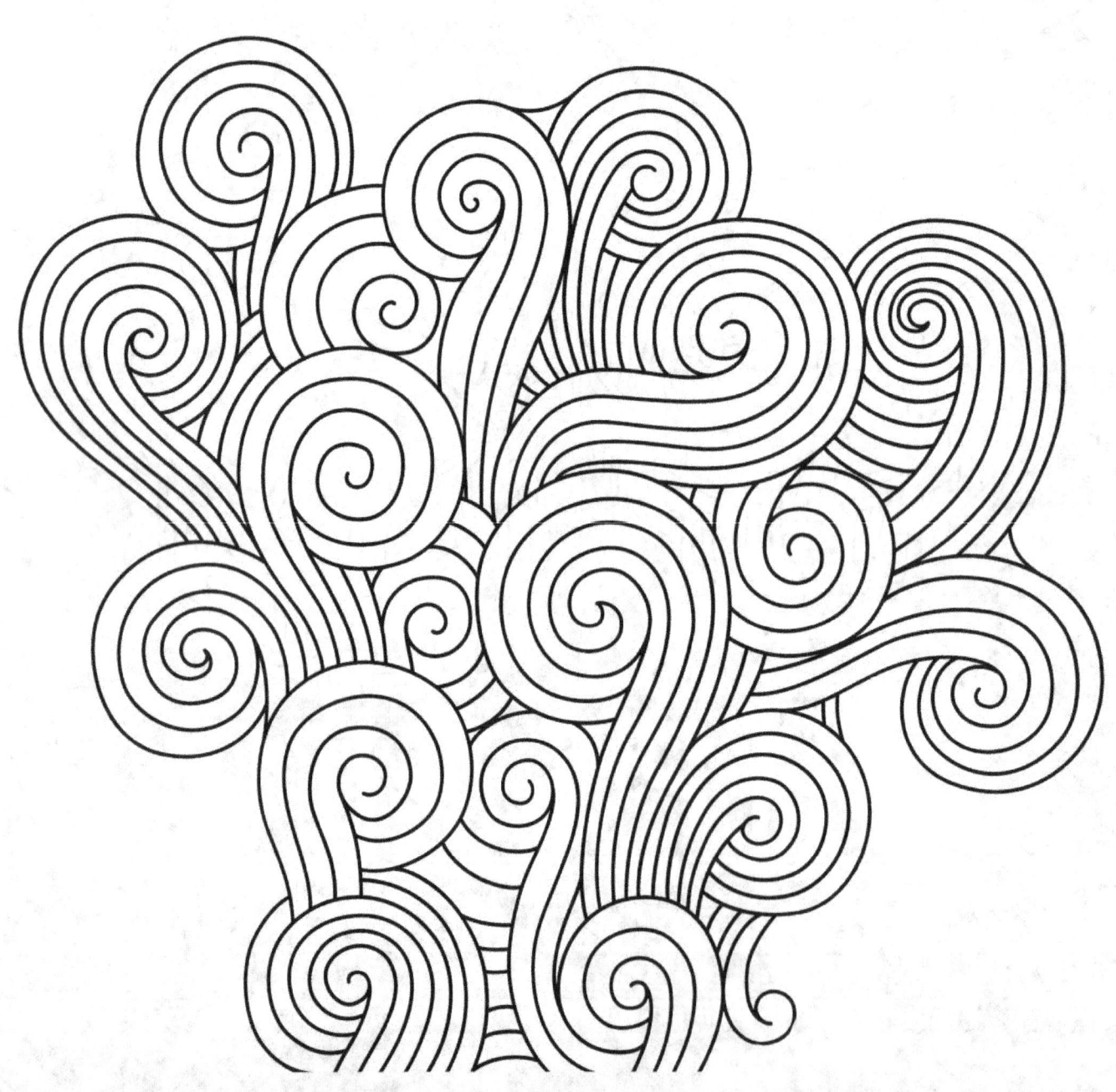

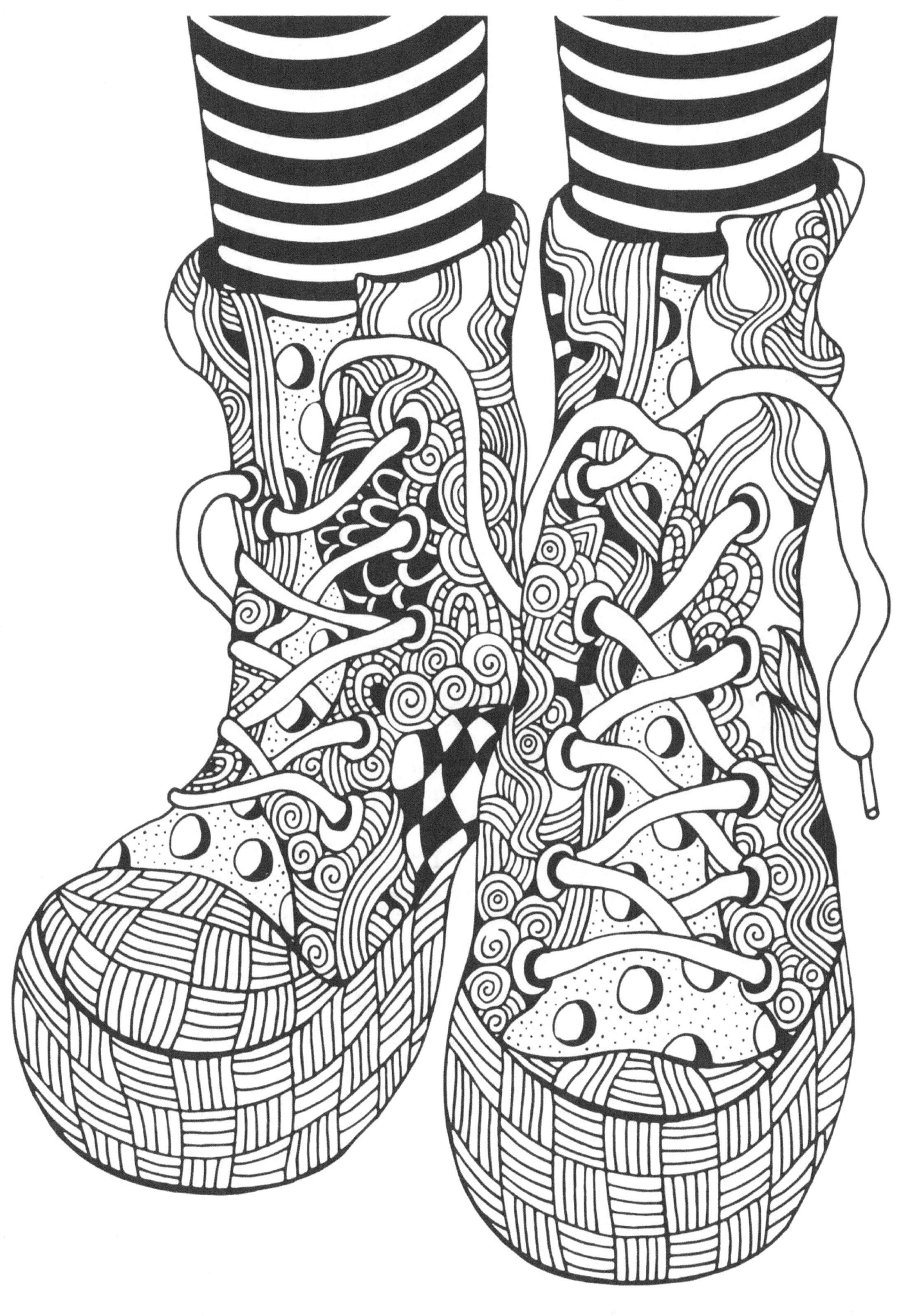

1.

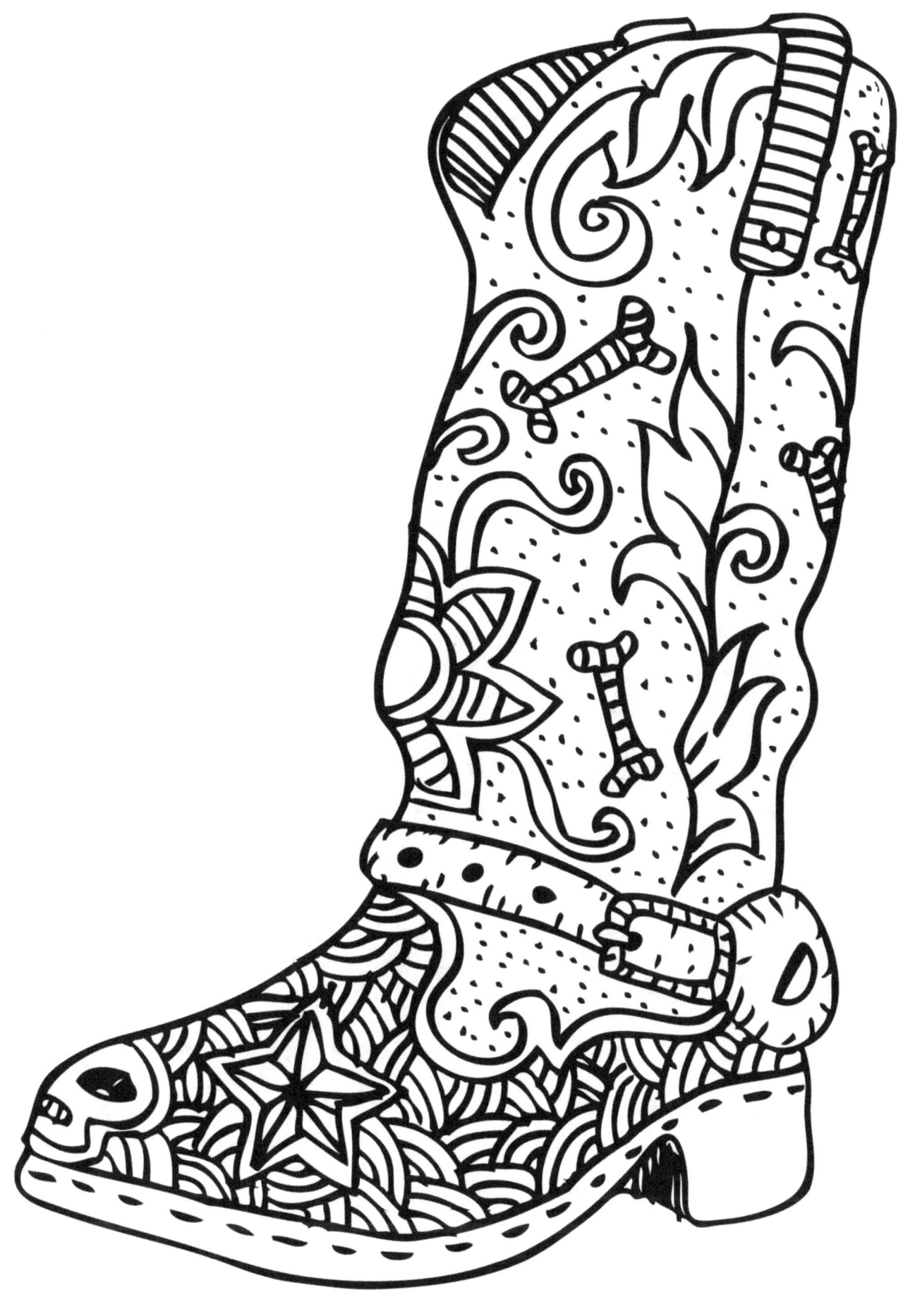

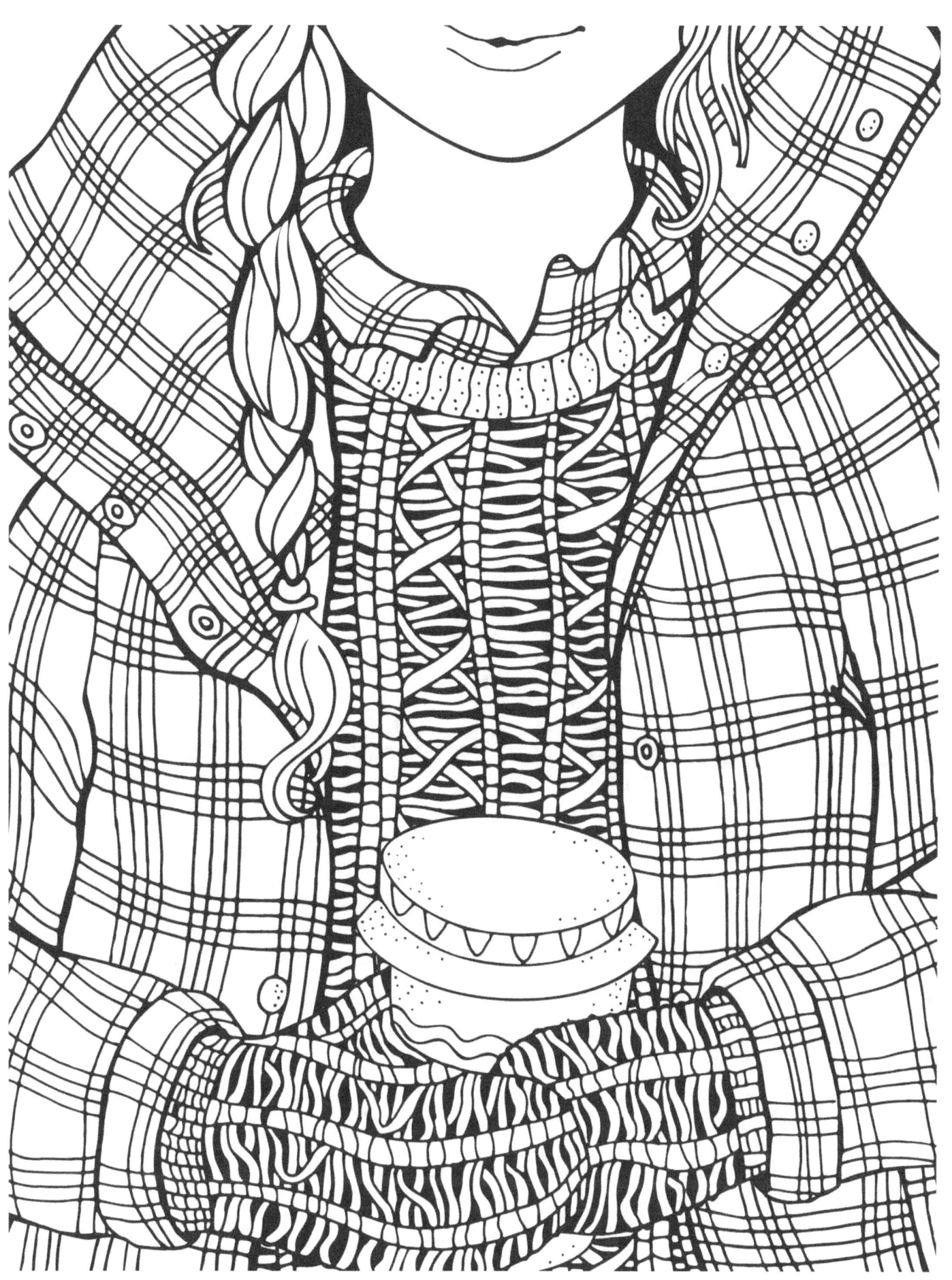

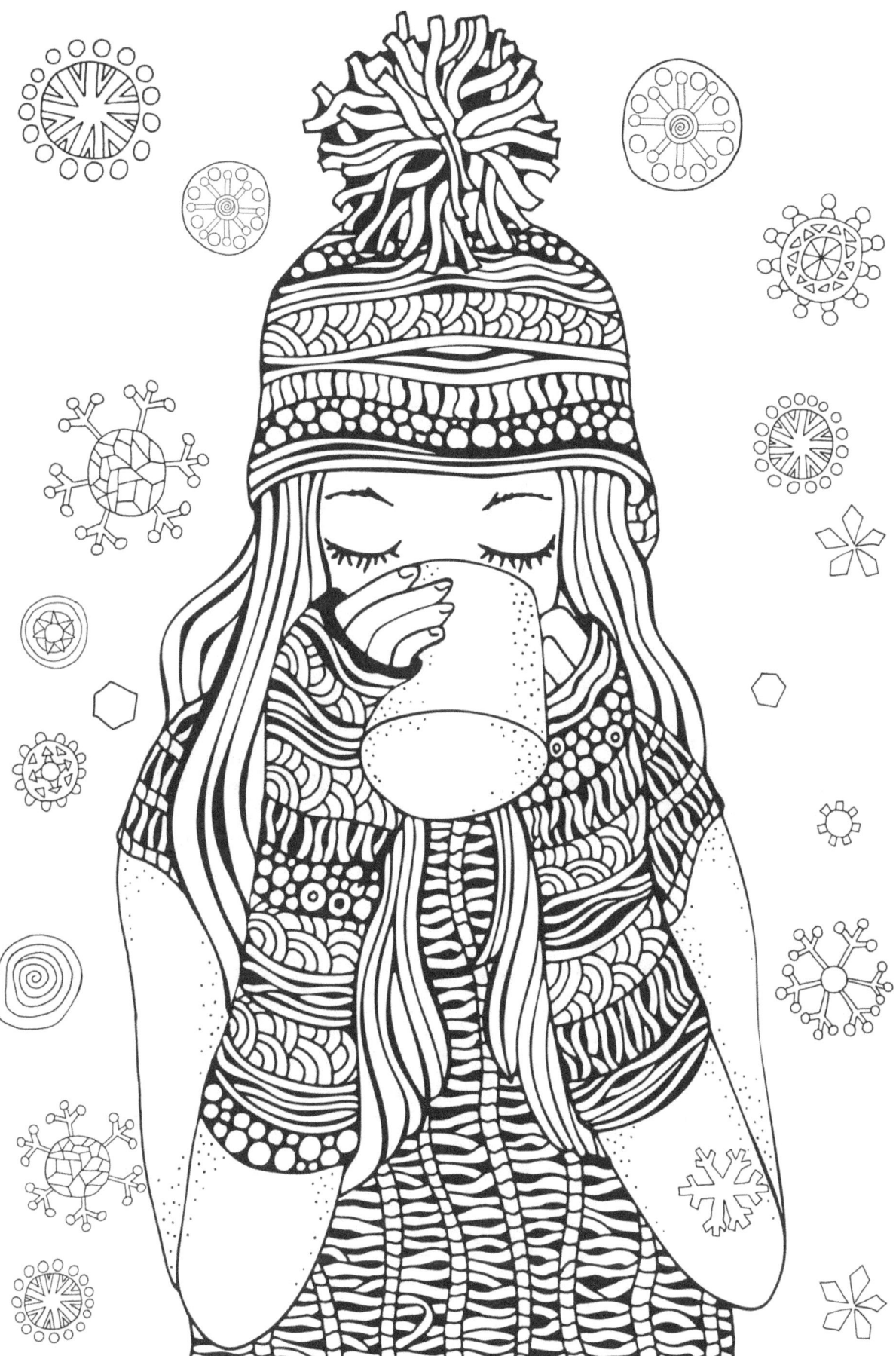

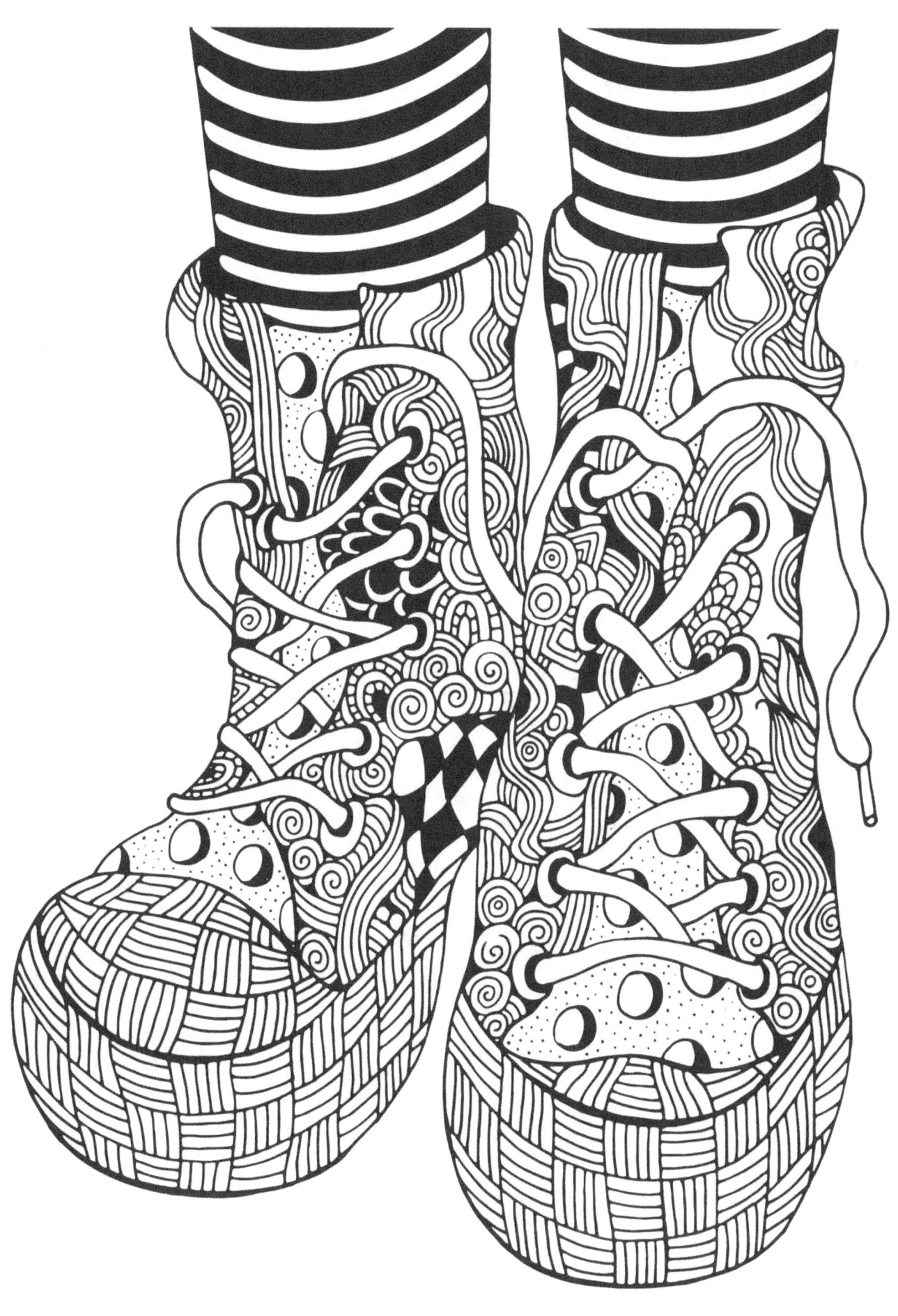

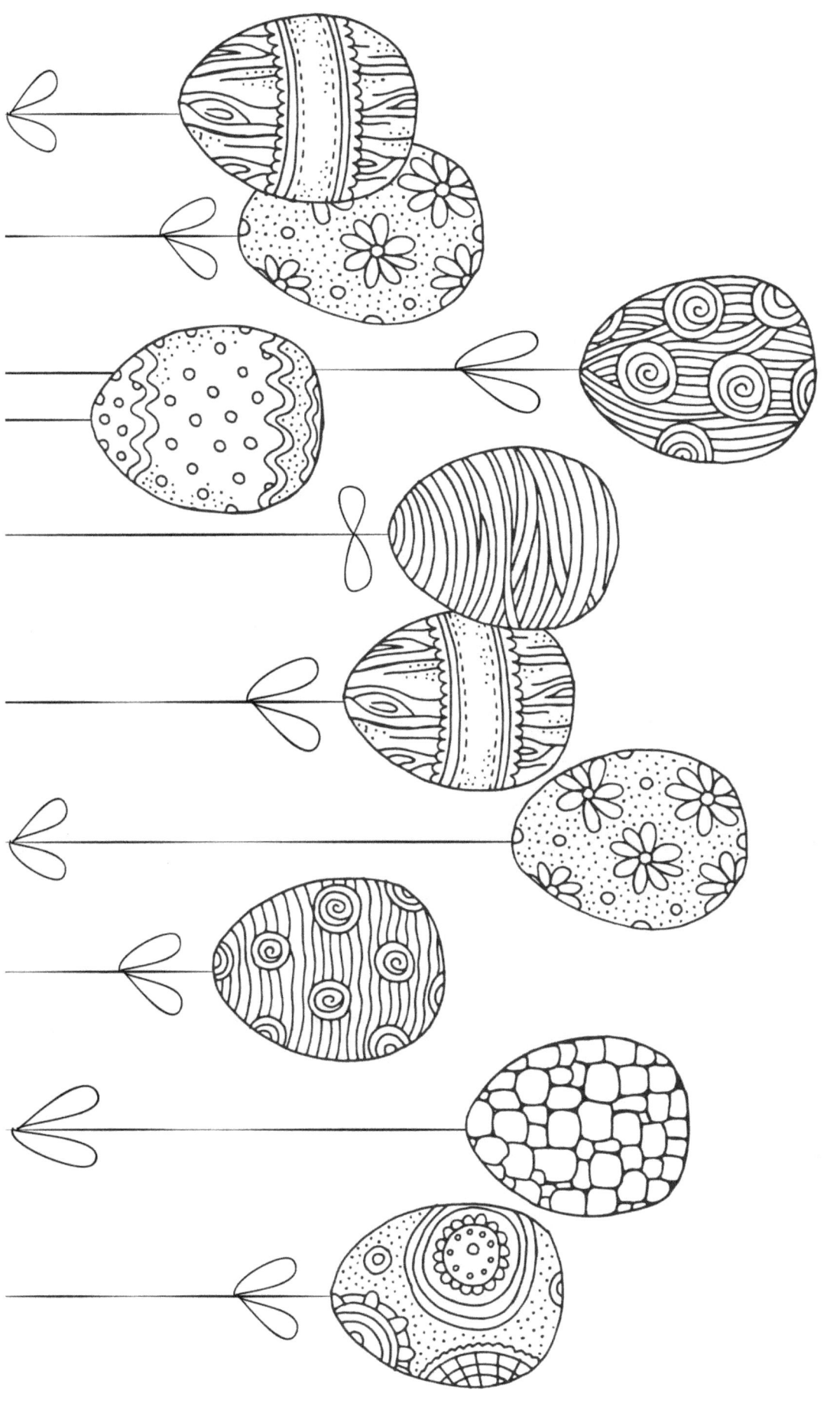

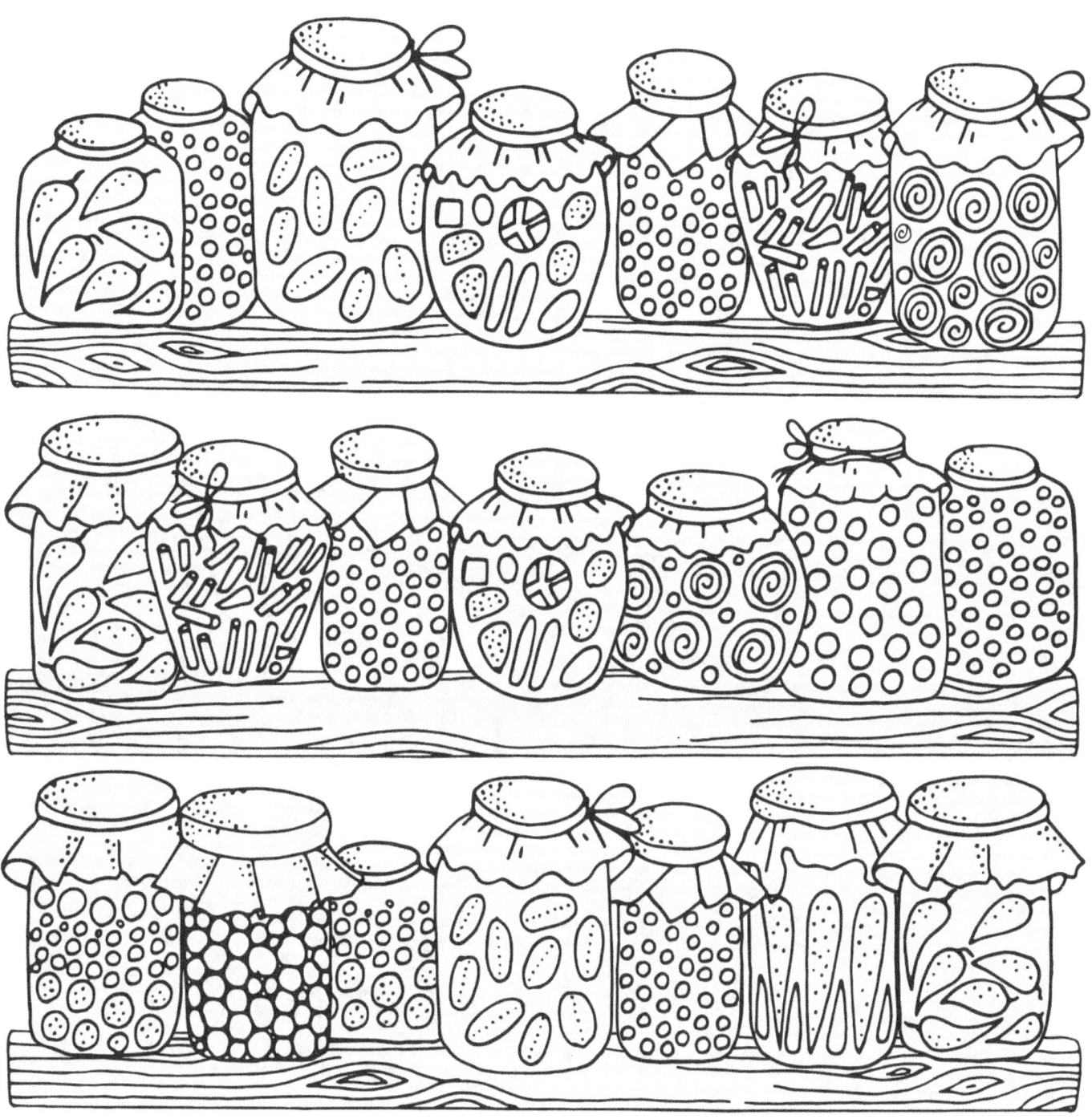

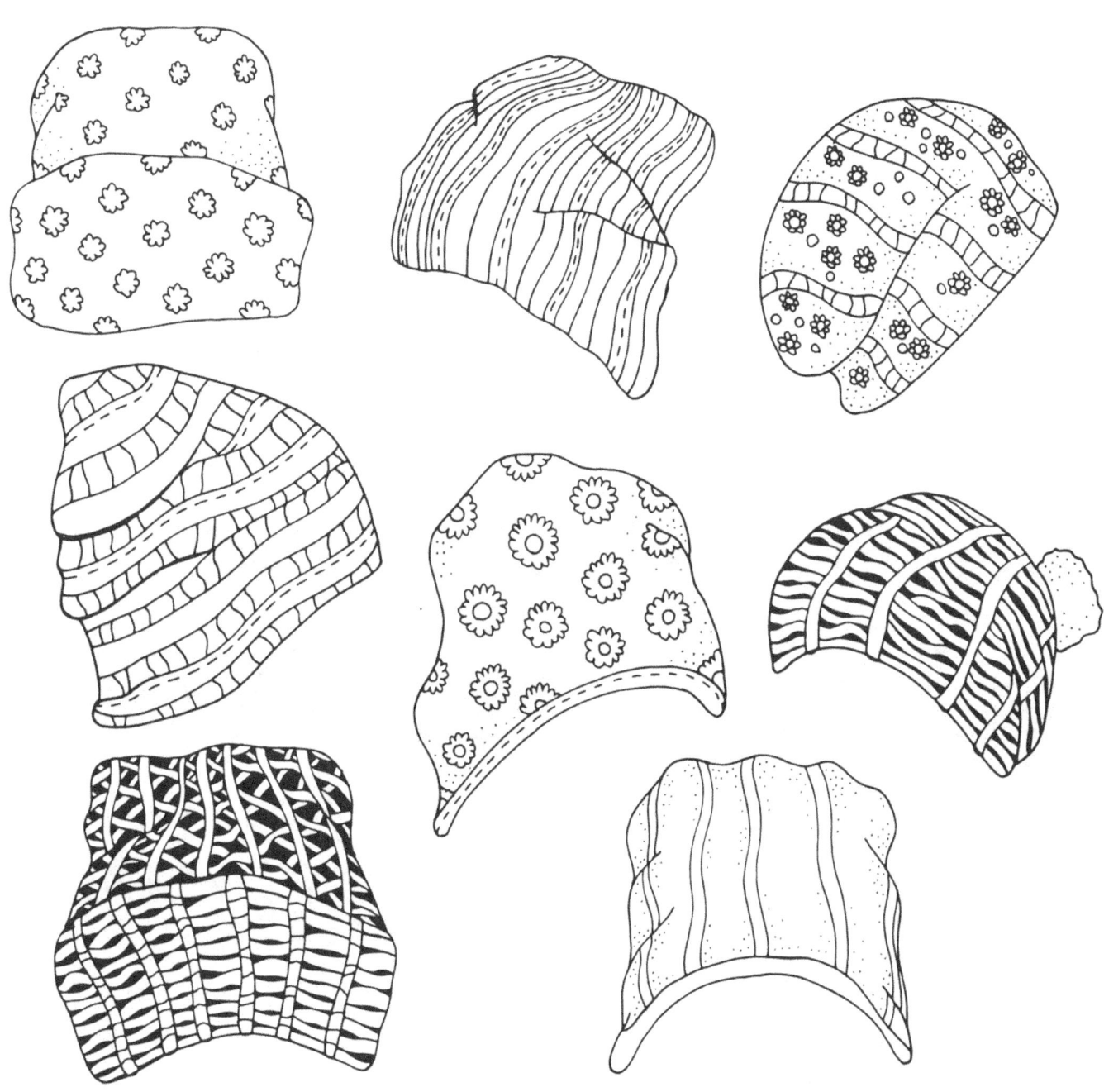

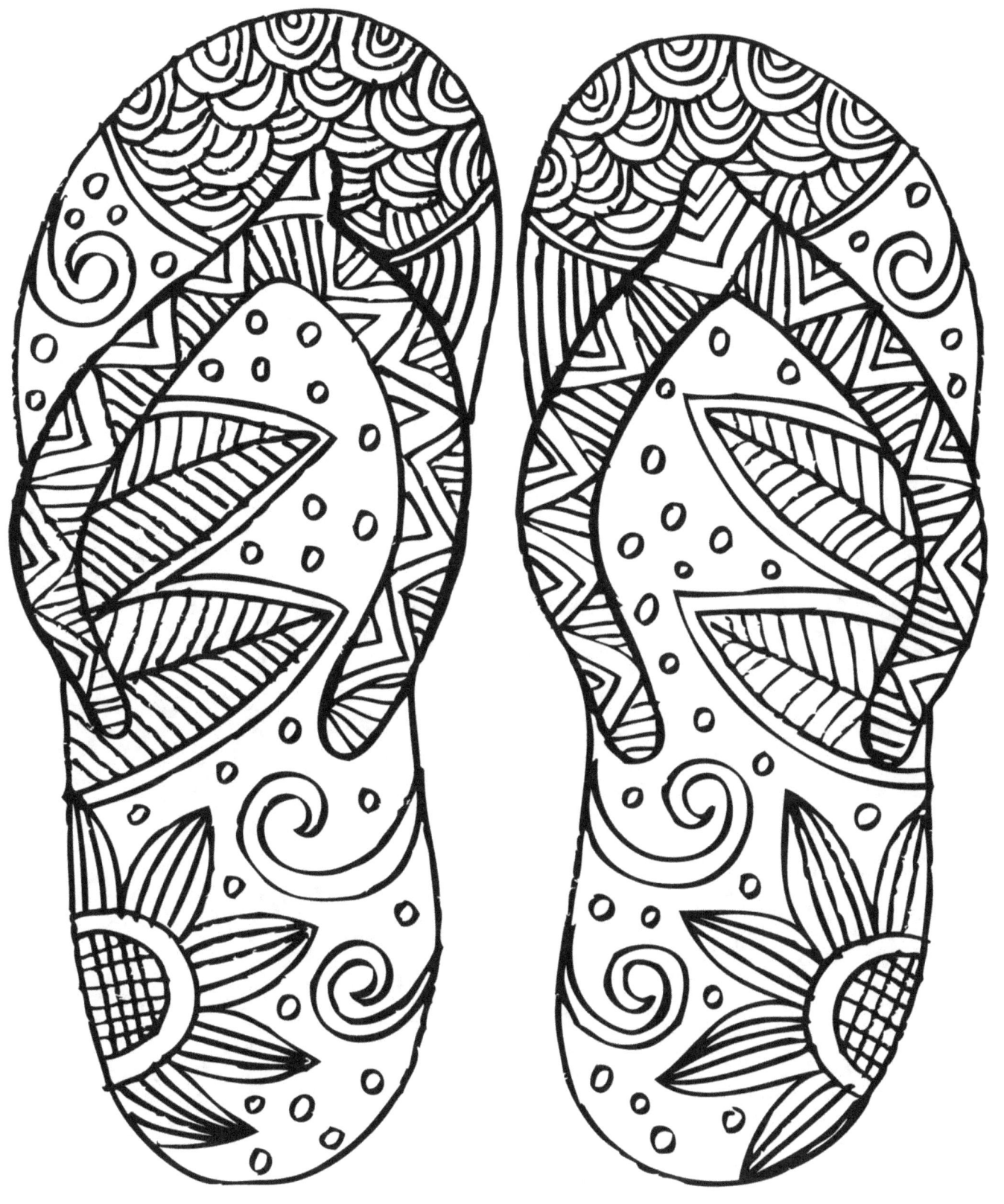

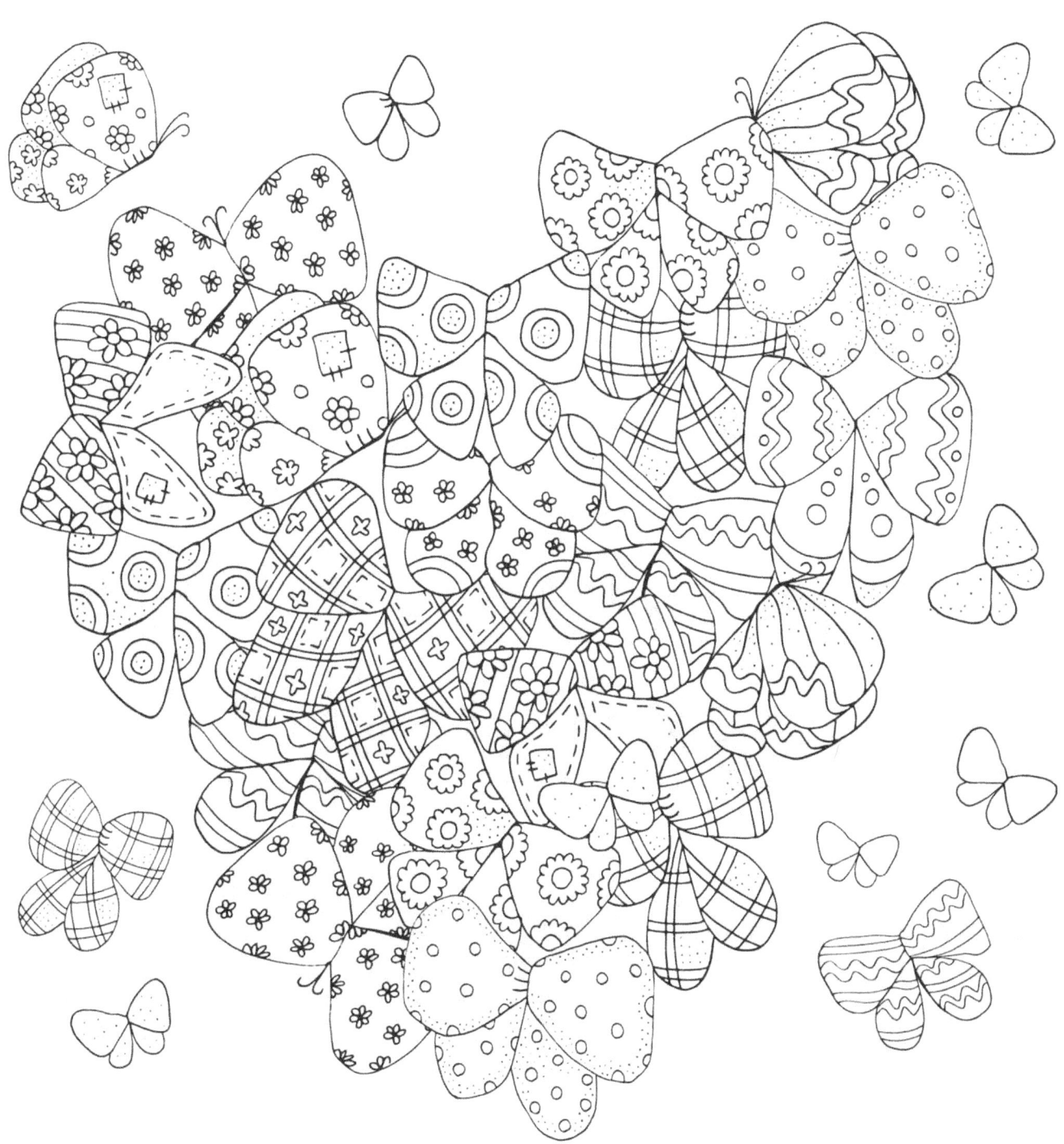

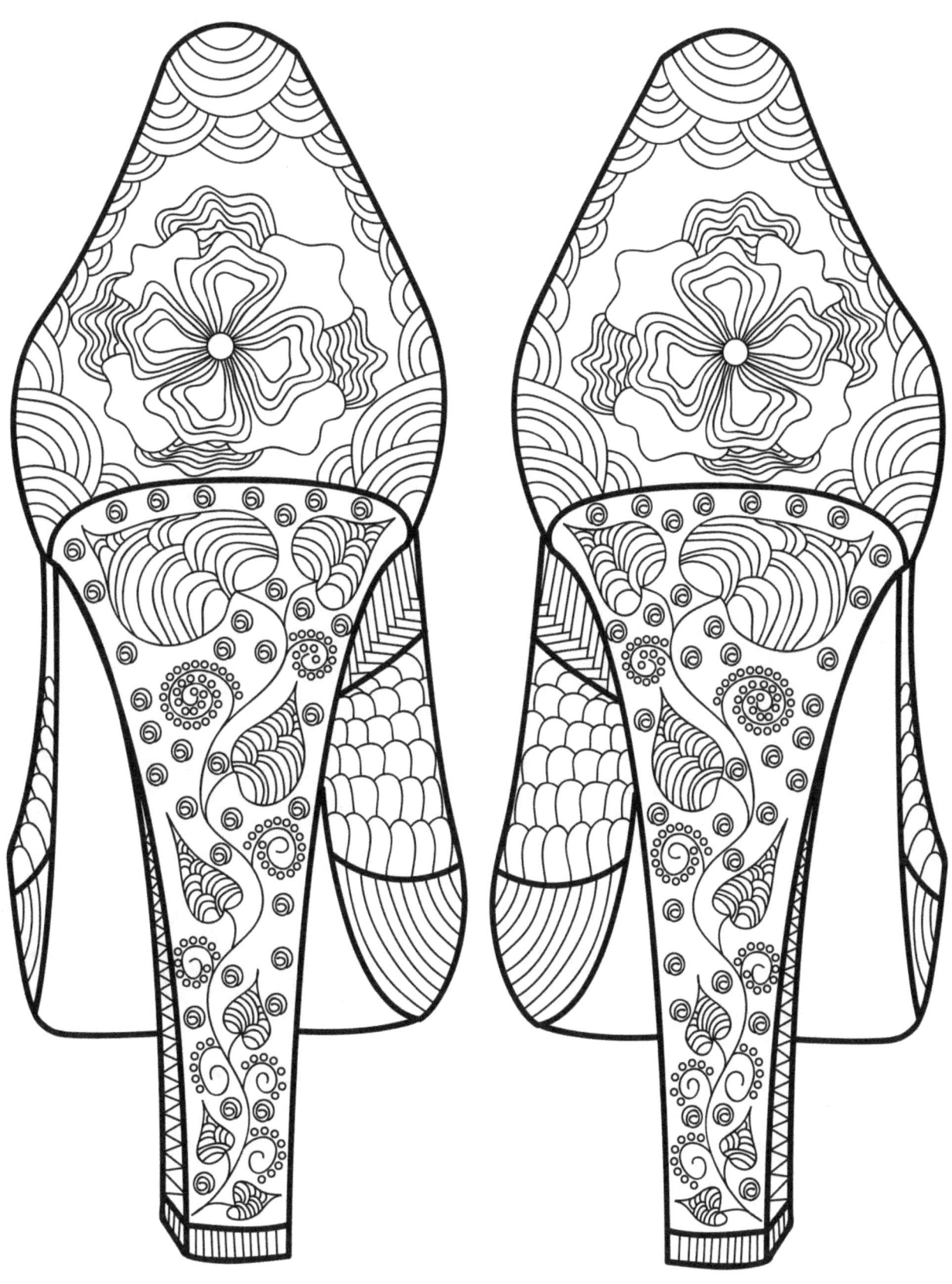

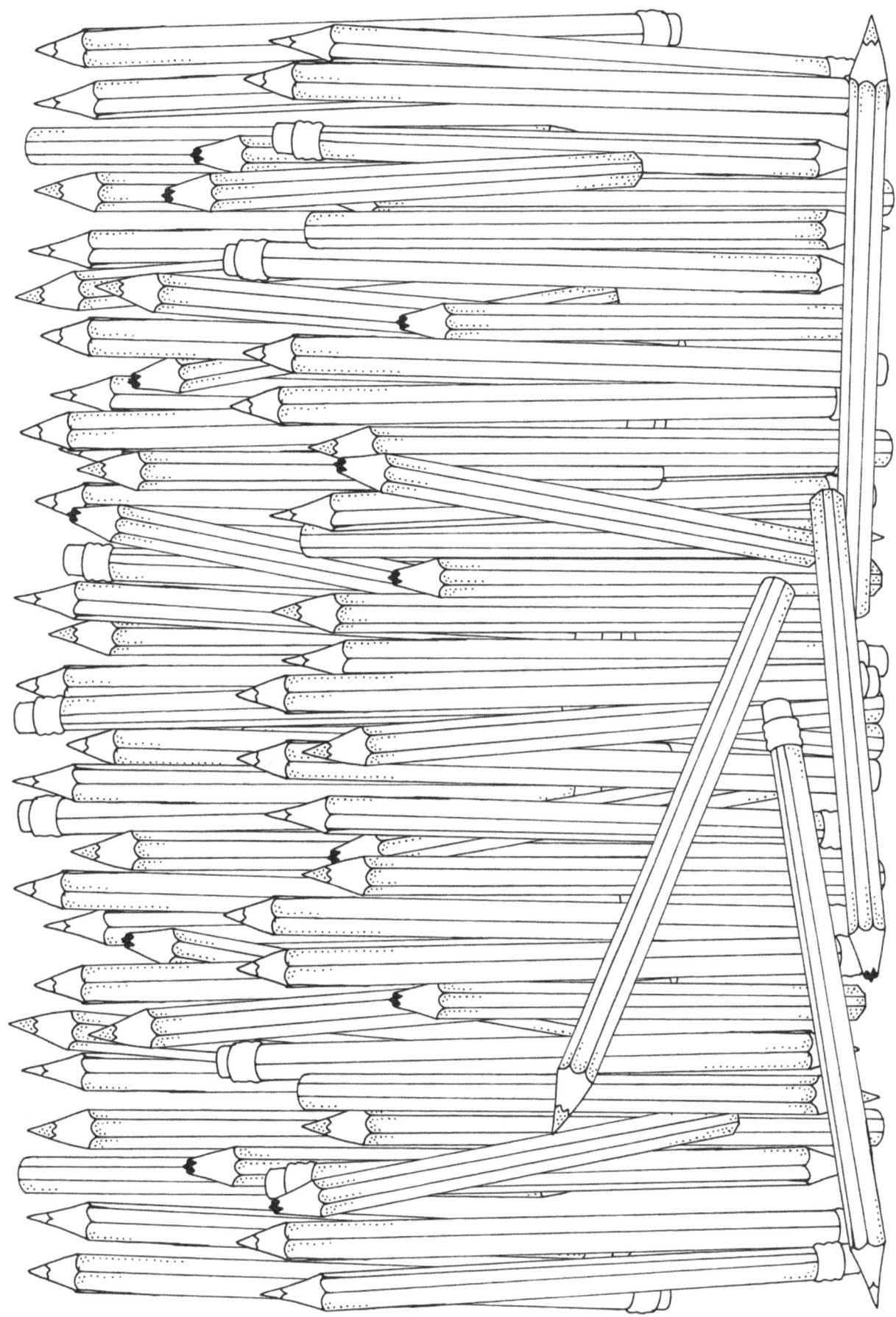

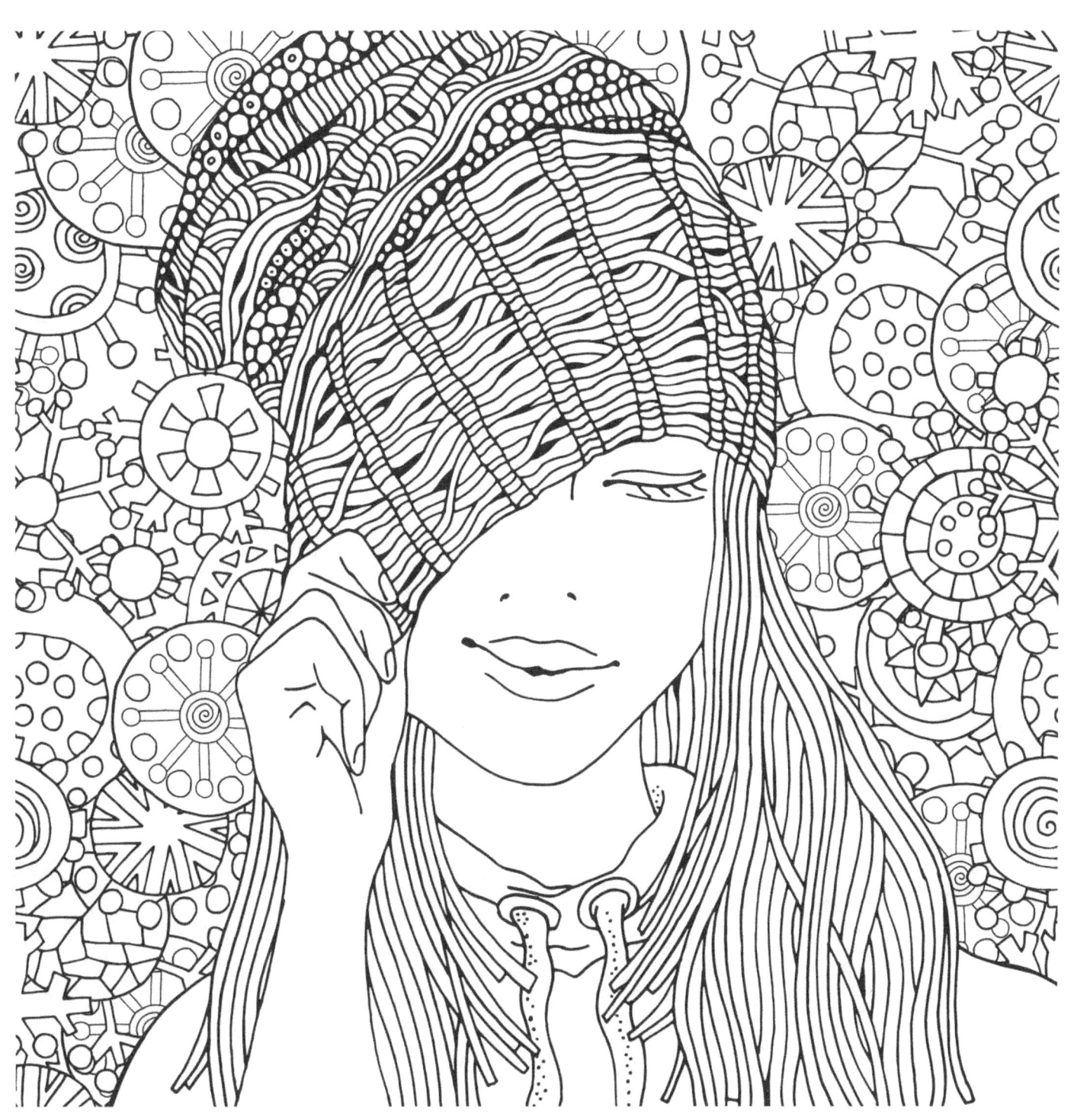

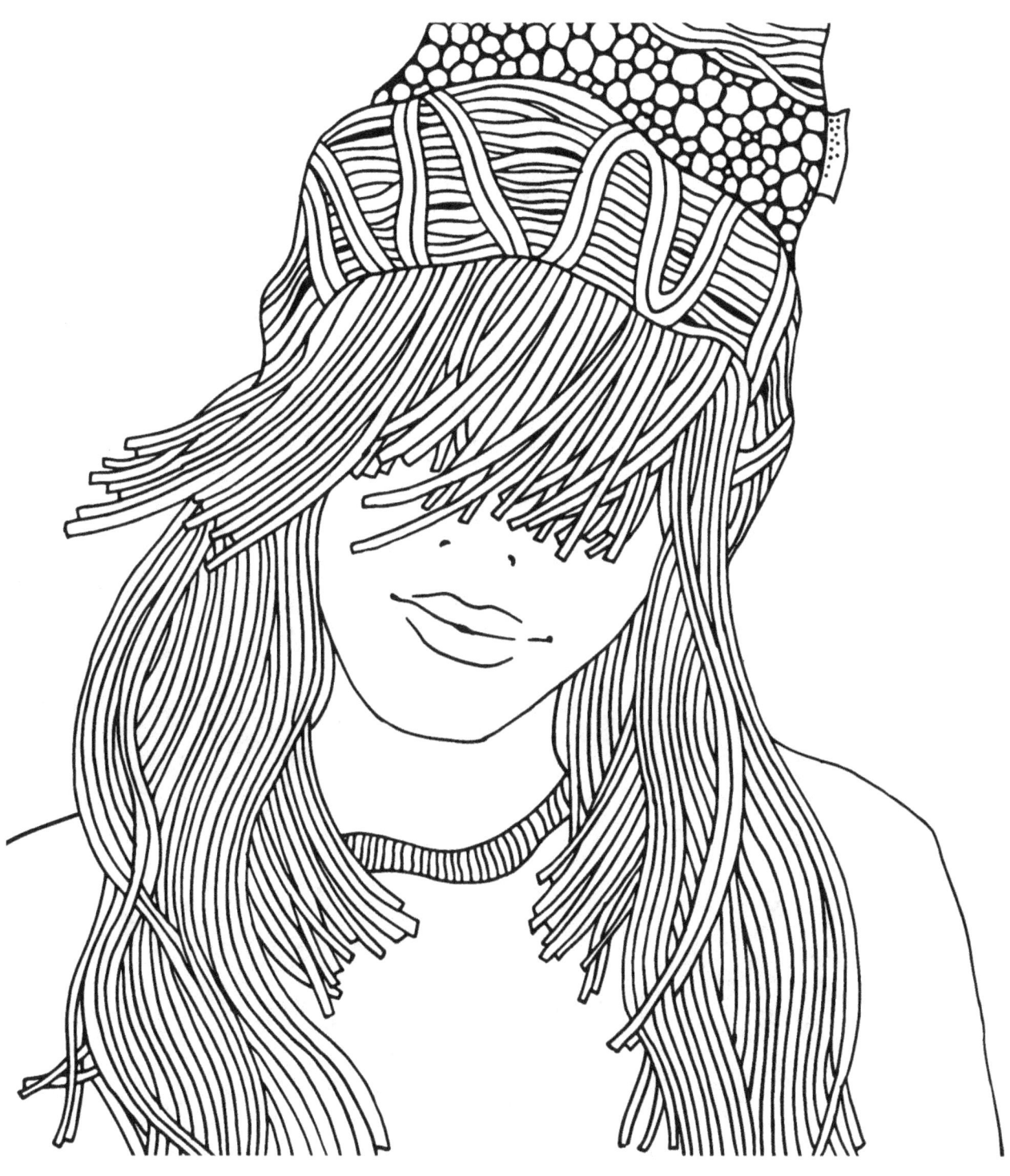

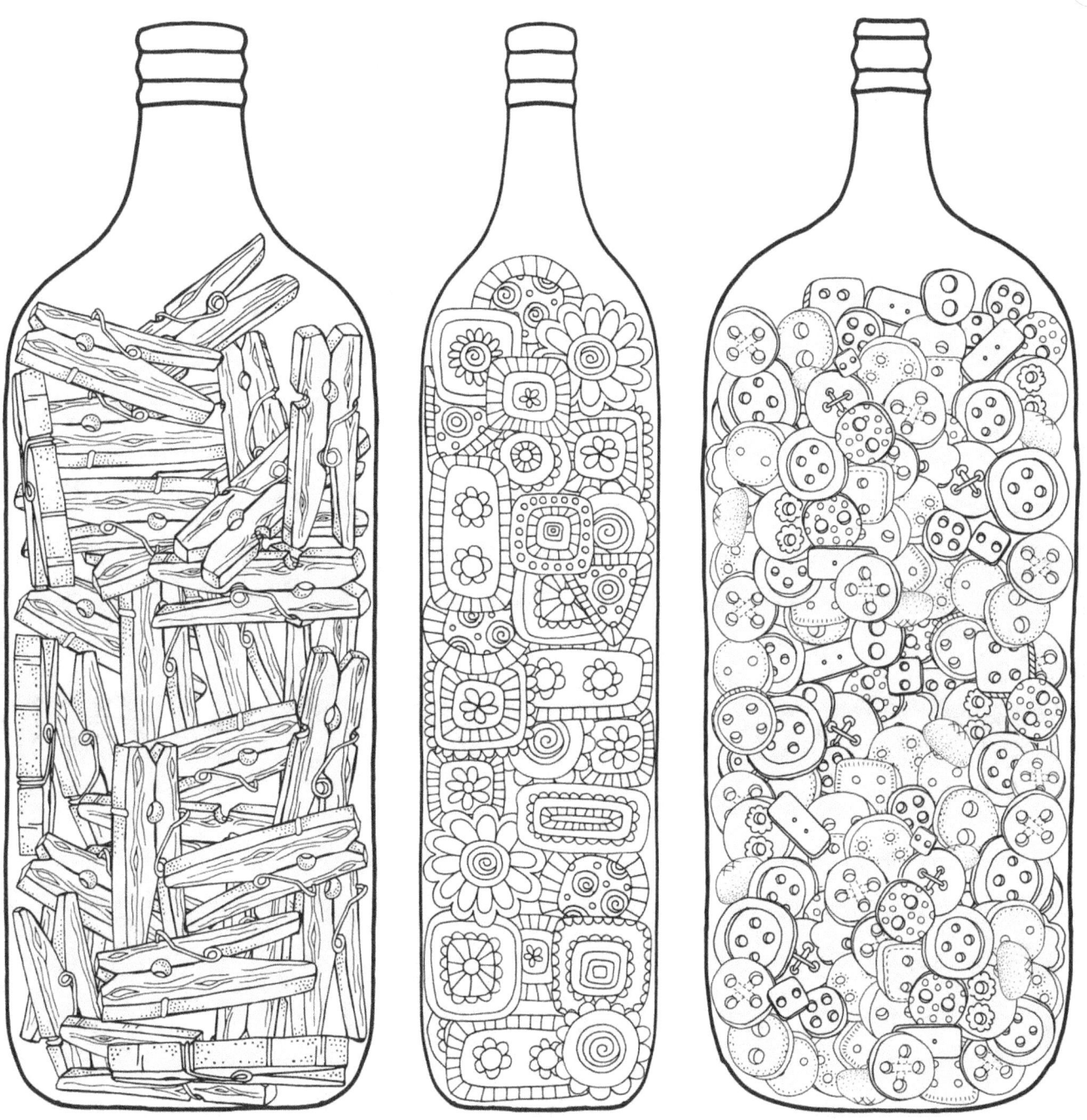

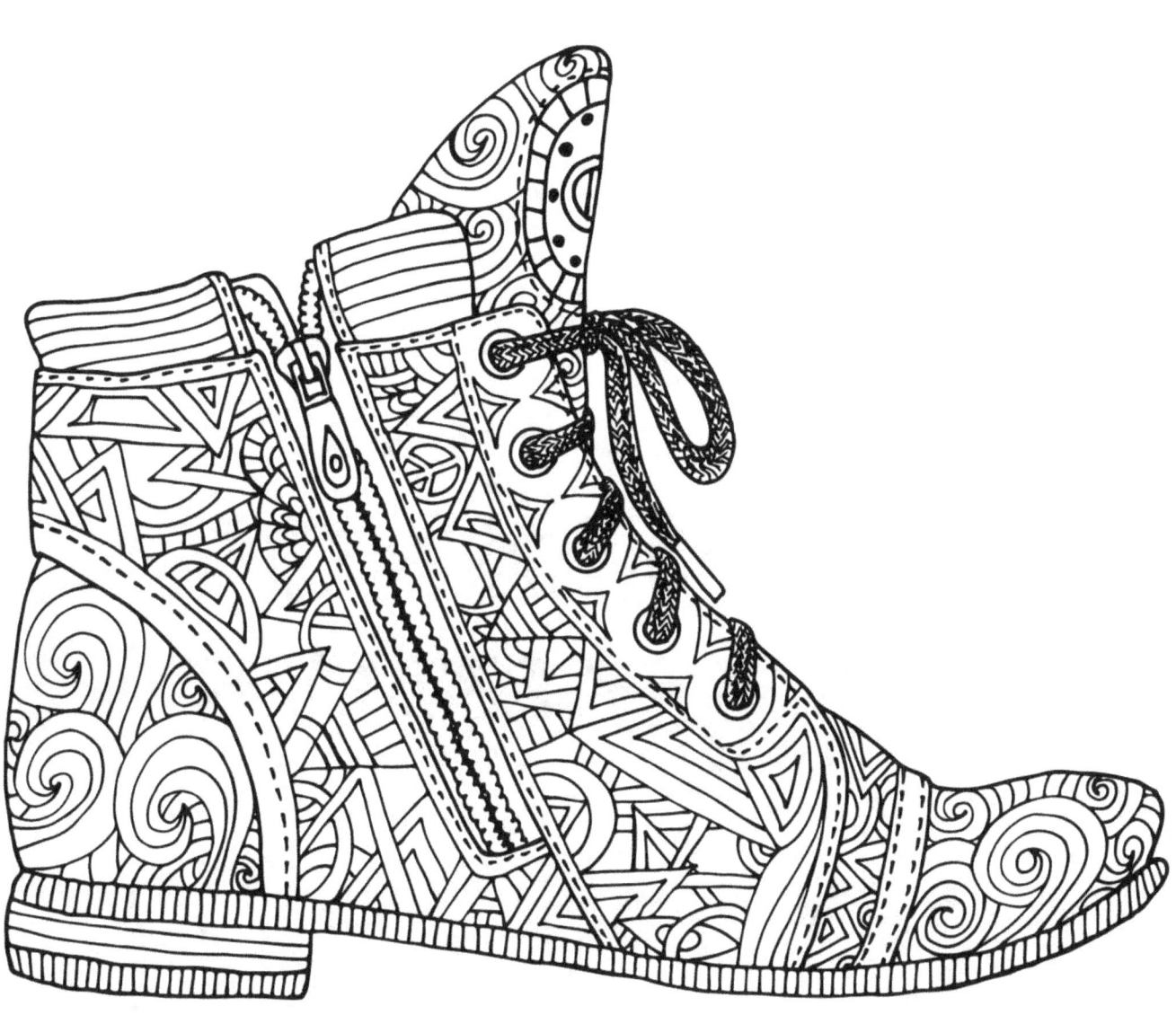

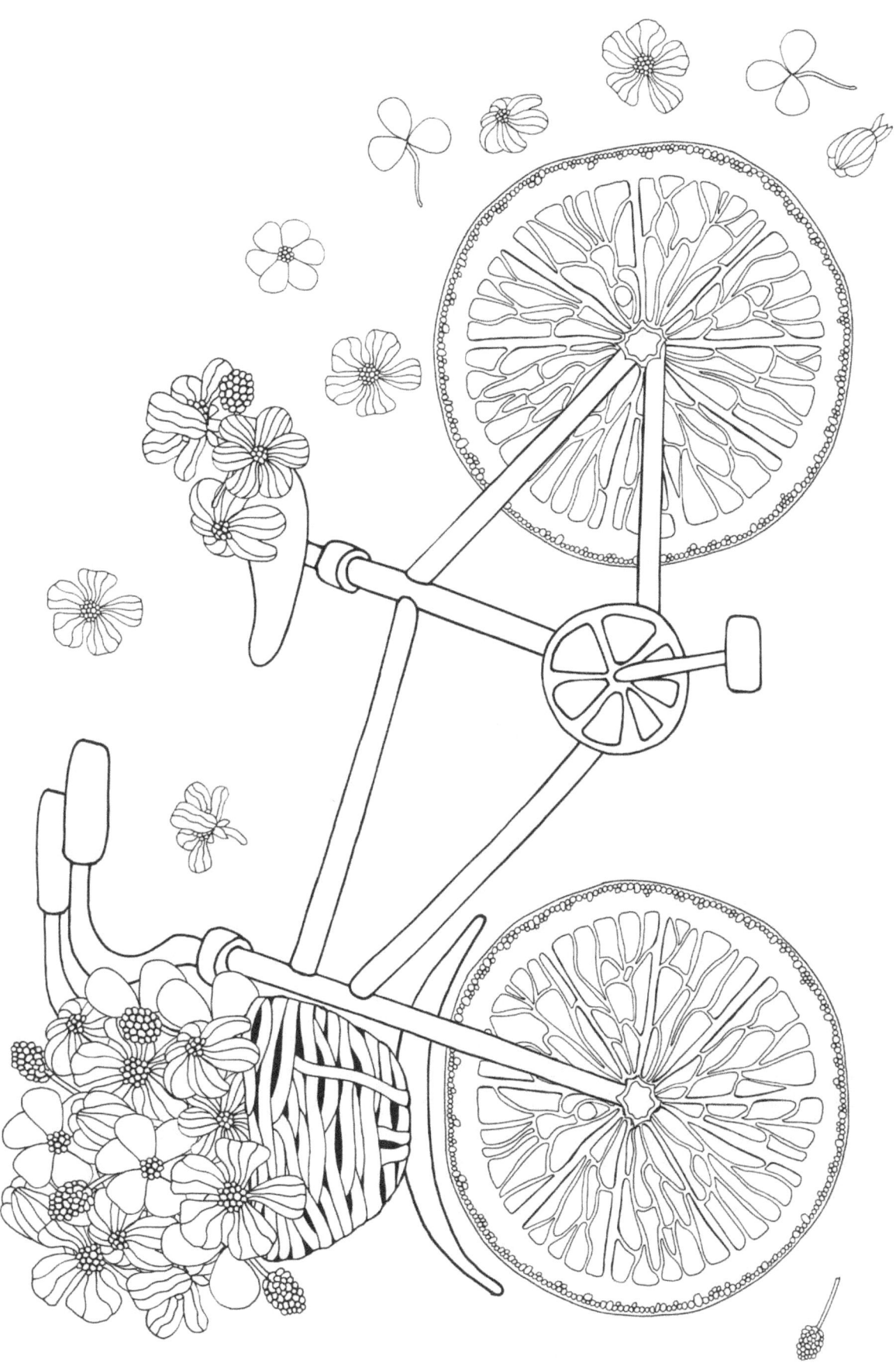

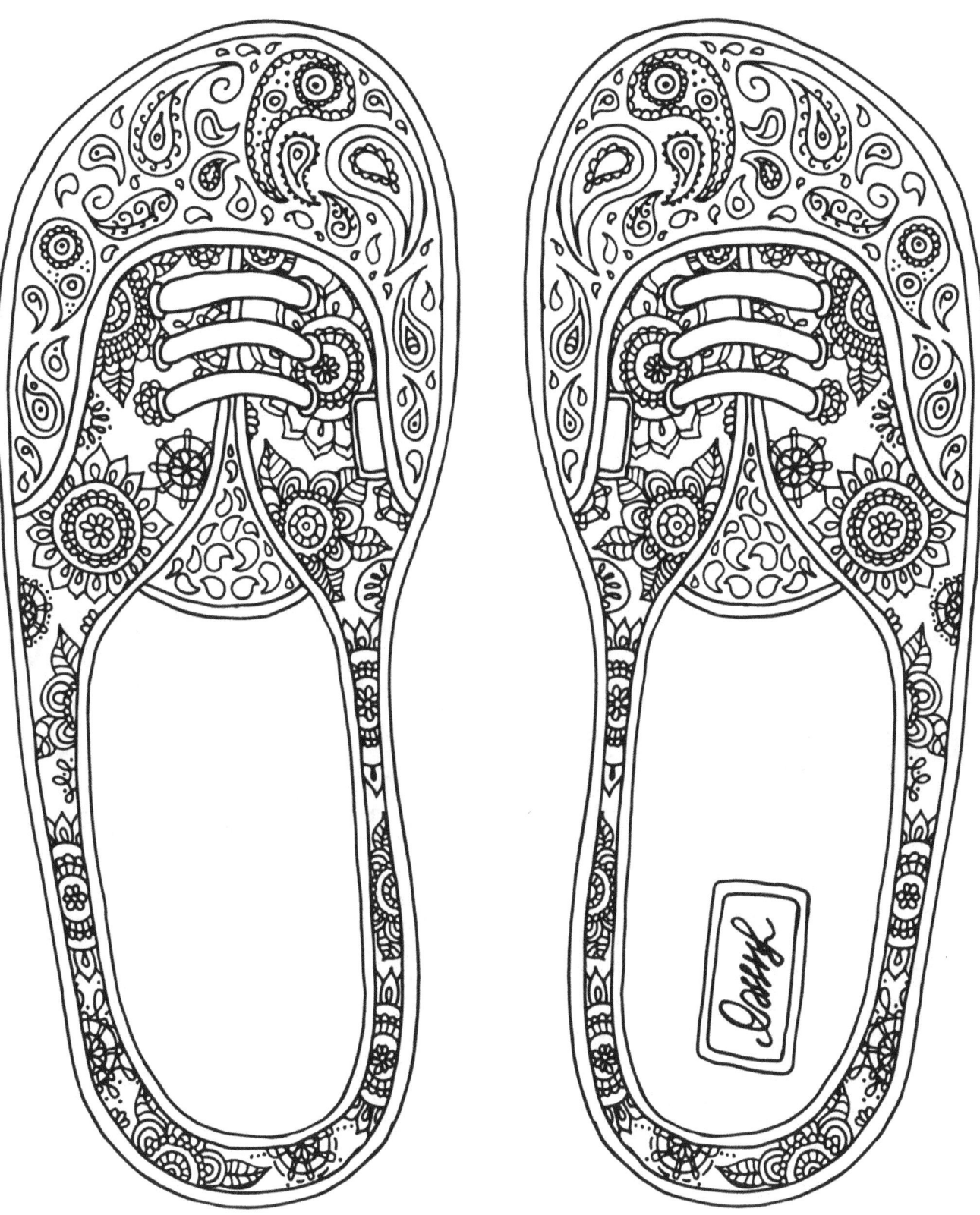

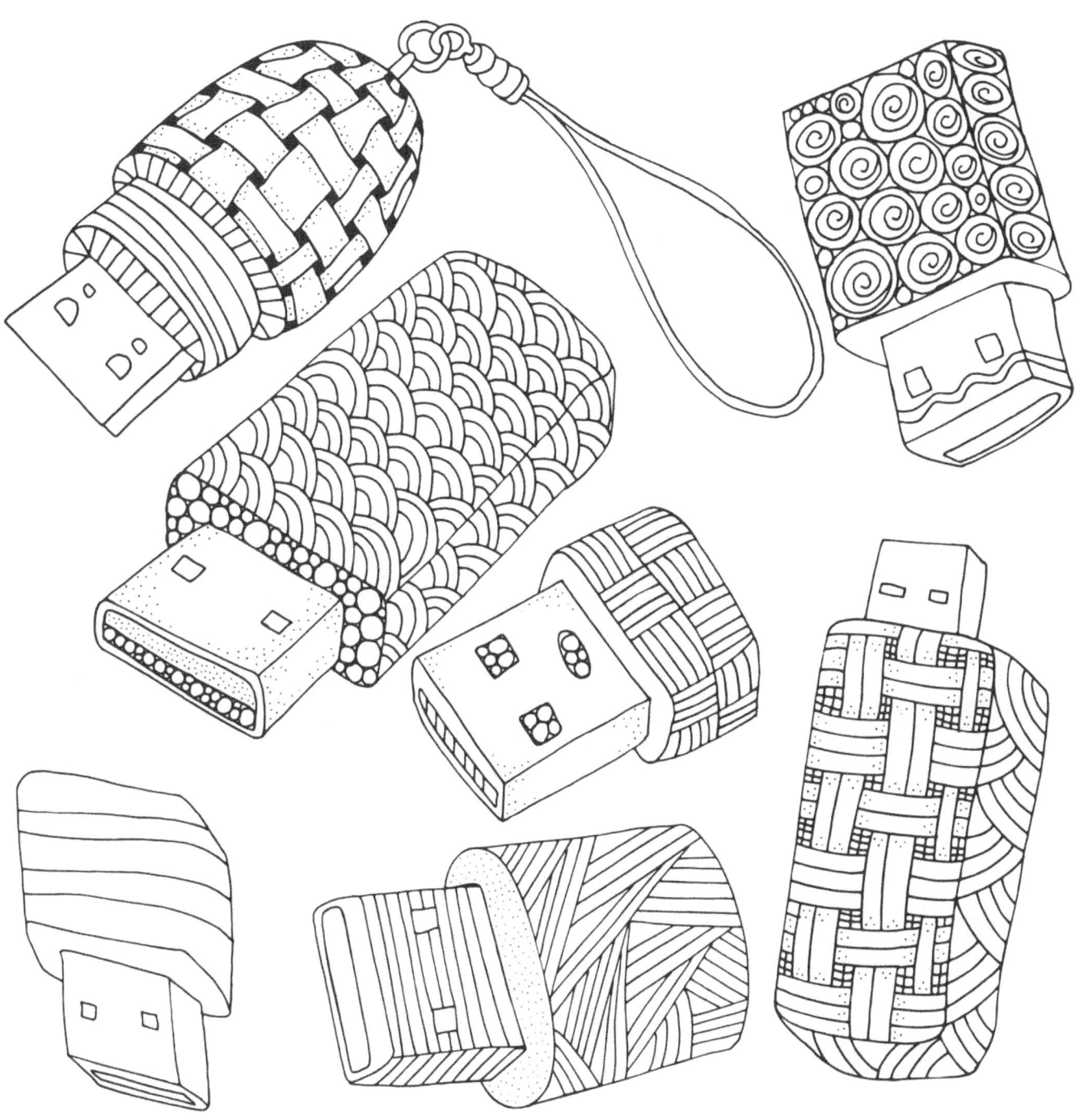

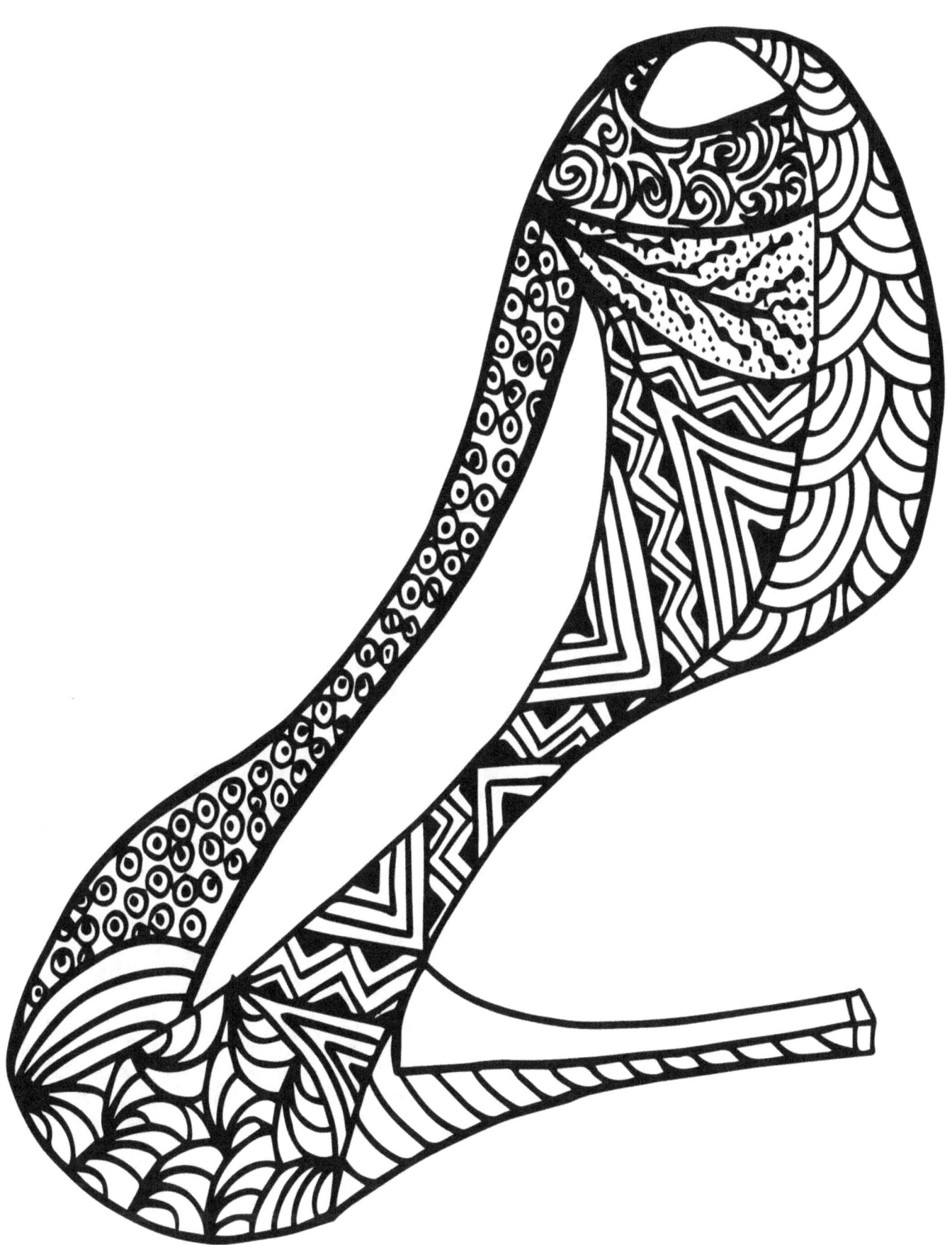

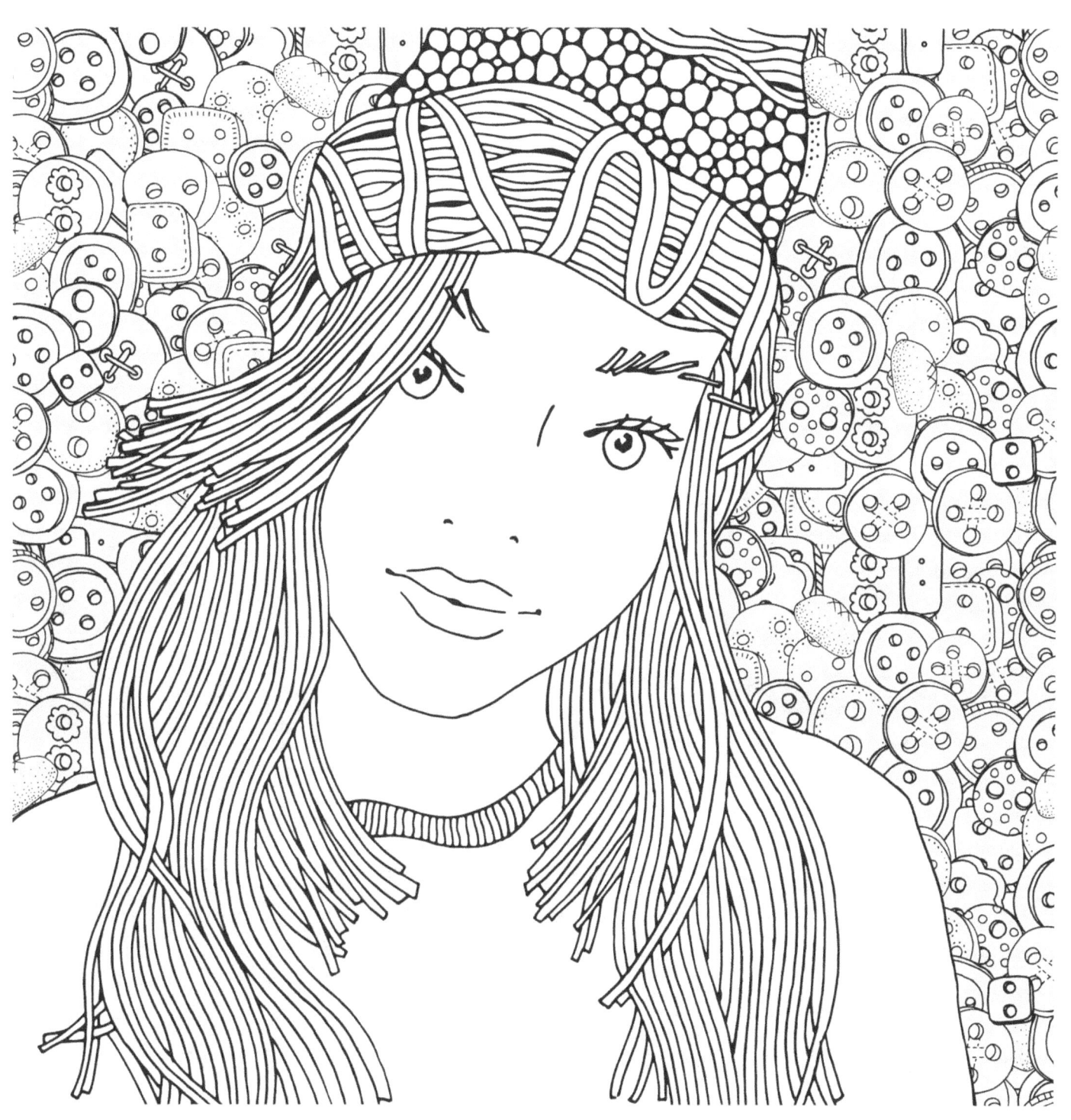

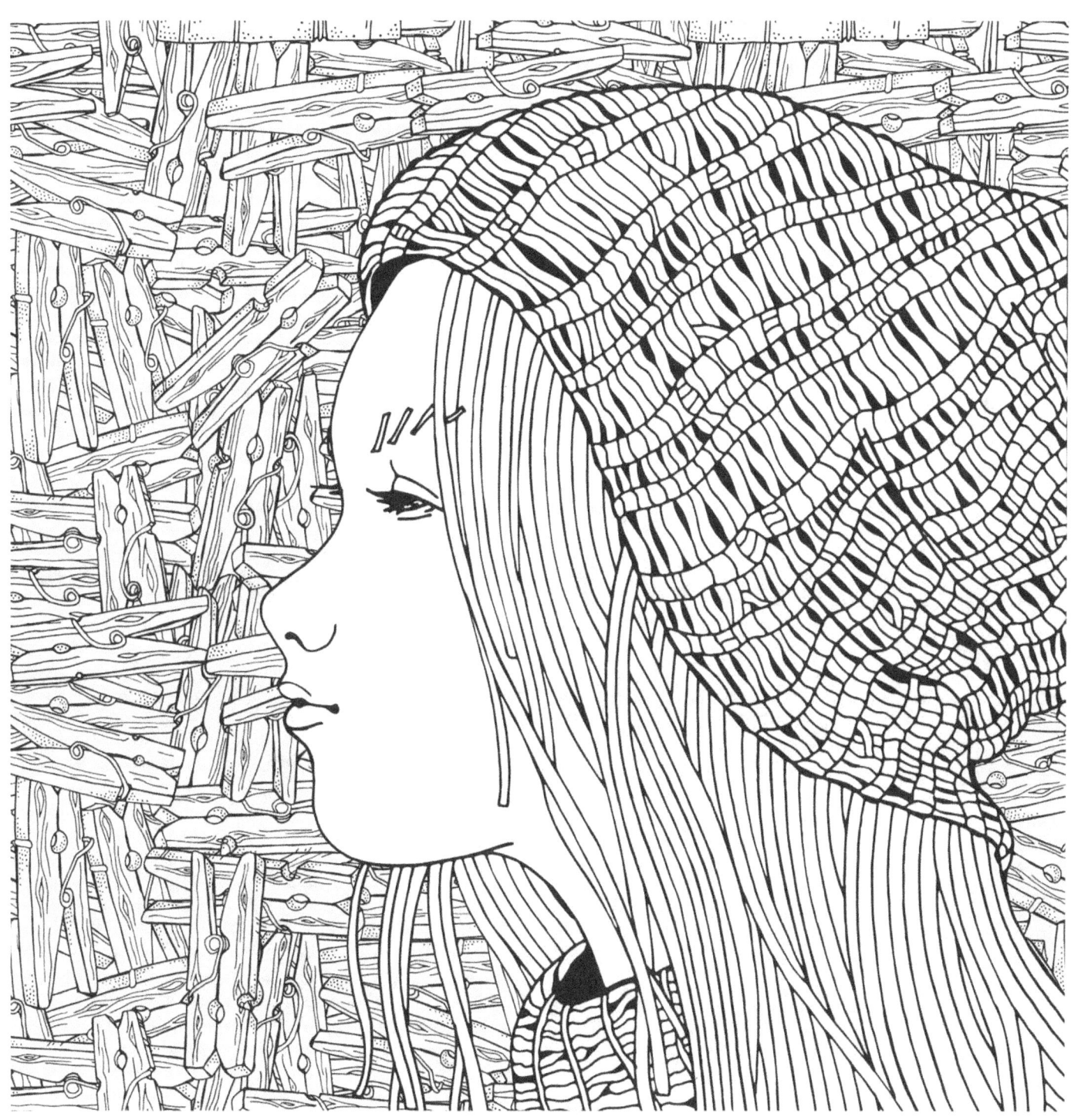

www.ingramcontent.com/pod-product-compliance
Lightning Source LLC
Chambersburg PA
CBHW081133180526
45170CB00008B/3090